The Little Book of Self-Compassion

KATHRYN LOVEWELL

The Little Book of Self-Compassion
First published in 2019 by
Kind Mind Publishing
East Drive, Carshalton Beeches, Surrey, SM5 4PB
Email: Liz@KindMindAcademy.com

Illustrations by Penny Haynes
www.BlueBeanCartoons.co.uk
Design & Artwork by Marta Dec
www.martadec.eu

Printed on acid-free paper from managed forests. This book is
printed on demand, so no copies will be remaindered or pulped.

ISBN 978-1-913045-04-3

With thanks to and warm recognition of Christopher
Germer and Kristin Neff who gave birth to the Mindful
Self-Compassion programme which has inspired this
humble little book and radically changed my inner life.

Dedicated to every member of the MSC community who have kindly contributed to my self-compassion adventure and who continue to help guide me to live a self-compassionate life.

With special thanks to Liz, Julia, Melony, Rianne and Tina.

With warm appreciation for Toolangi Heights and it's kind custodians.

Forever grateful.

Acknowledgement

From as young as I can remember I had a fierce inner critic. There was no escaping my very high standards and expectations of how I *should* behave. Even if I simply thought an unkind thought I would beat myself up for being a 'bad girl'. Throughout my life I tried desperately hard to be a good person, do my best, work earnestly and help others as much as I could. Sadly, I never gave myself a break for making mistakes, being ill, feeling sensitive or not understanding something.

All this changed when I learned Mindful Self-Compassion. Mindful Self-Compassion (MSC) is an empirically supported, 8-week, programme based on ground breaking research by Kristin Neff, PhD, and the clinical expertise of Christopher Germer, PhD. MSC teaches core principles and skills that enable us to respond to difficult situations and emotions with the same compassion we would extend to our loved ones. *The Little Book of Self-Compassion* is inspired by this ground-breaking programme.

See Appendix A for specific practices and exercises gently adapted for this little book.

Because MSC so dramatically changed my internal life I trained to teach their programme. I qualified as a certified teacher and continue to deepen my practice within the MSC community. This little book is a warm bow to Chris and Kristin's pioneering work. I hope it has captured some of MSC's key principles in a simple and accessible way; so that if you are feeling overwhelmed, crushed by your critical voice, time starved or maybe even hopeless and helpless, this introduction will be the first step to a new way of life.

Since the first day I began MSC, I have moved closer and closer to a kinder life inside my own skin. I hope this little stepping stone will inspire you to embrace the full programme one day. Then you too can learn to be kind to yourself no matter what you have done or not done. You are worthy of love and self-kindness.

Be careful what you say to yourself, you might be listening!

Just so you know...

This is NOT a self-improvement book... If you are looking to fix or change yourself because you believe you are flawed, broken or incomplete, this little book looks at things rather differently. However, keep reading, because with a self-compassionate approach to yourself and your life, you can begin to make friends with all the things you believe need fixing and bring a kinder more supportive approach to yourself and your situation instead.

This is a little book of kindness guiding you back to your heart. There you will uncover all the loving kindness, strength, compassion and acceptance that you need to make friends with the very precious person reading this book.

The Little Book of Self-Compassion opens the door to loving and accepting yourself just as you are, warts and all, rather than striving to fix, change or better yourself.

> *"It's not your job to like me, it's mine!"*
>
> Byron Katie

If you feel very resistant to this idea, you're not alone. When I embarked on living a self-compassionate life, all I wanted was to get rid of my self-loathing, stop hating my body and be a confident person. In my mind, there was a LOT to fix. In my skewed view, I was a mess! Not necessarily on the outside, but there was still a great deal of conflict and dissatisfaction with myself on the inside.

This little book, which is written with so much tenderness and compassion, is a gentle introduction to living and breathing self-compassion in your everyday life. If I could have taken a 'before and after' photo of my inner landscape, wow, you would really see a significant difference!

I am now shiny on the inside. I am kind on the inside. I am even a little more patient on the inside! I have learnt to make friends with my critical voice (which, by the way, was reeeeally mean) and I can meet whatever 'brown stuff' shows up with as much kindness as I can, as best I can, in each moment.

Final word about this non-fixing approach... I am human. I make mistakes. I still struggle sometimes. Whilst I would love to say that my self-compassion practice has brought nothing but shiny unicorns and sparkly rainbows into my world, I cannot. I still make the occasional blunder. I still find life pretty tough sometimes. I still experience self-doubt and waning confidence when I am out of my comfort zone.

The difference now, is that, when I struggle, I can be kind to myself. When I have a tough day, I am kind to myself. When I am in pain, I am kind to myself. When I fail at something, I am kind to myself. No matter what is going on, I have the skills and ability to give myself what I need and that begins with being kind.

Join me! Self-compassion is an epic adventure. It will take you to untrodden territory. It will be like no journey you have ever embarked upon. Get ready for the ride of your life. It really is worth taking and this book is just the beginning. Simply approach these pages with an open mind, a sense of adventure and with kind curiosity, as best you can!

Know that you are loved and even if your heart feels barricaded up right now, I promise there is a way to gently melt your armour and unlock the door to your own beautiful, precious heart. Come with me now...

"A moment of
self-compassion can
change your entire day...

...a string of such moments can change the course of your life."

Christopher Germer

Soothing Soup

The best and easiest way to understand the gift of self-compassion, what it is and what it isn't, is by applying what I like to call the soothing soup analogy.

Remember when you got the flu as a child or had some bug that made you feel yucky? There was nothing any doctor could really do about getting rid of your germs. Perhaps there was no medicine that could fix the ailment, you just had to wait it out. Even though you were under the weather, hopefully there was someone who would do their best to soothe you, to help you feel better, even if they couldn't make your body better in that moment.

If you weren't soothed or taken care of by a loving parent or carer in such a moment, perhaps you can imagine how being brought some soothing soup to help you feel better, would have felt. Perhaps you have become the kind parent or good friend who has since brought your child or friend something warming to help ease them when feeling poorly?

Now does your grandma's favourite recipe get rid of the bugs making you feel bad? Of course not! But does the act of receiving the soup that has been lovingly made for you, warm you, soothe you and maybe make you feel a little bit better, even though your condition hasn't changed. Yes, it does!

Self-Compassion is soothing soup. It doesn't aim to 'fix' the problem, but it does serve to soothe and comfort you when things are difficult.

Does this stop us from wanting the difficult situation (the germs) to go away? No. It simply helps us meet the difficulty with kindness and supports us in the moment of struggle. We become the kind parent, carer or friend that wants to ease our suffering, bring reassurance, support and solace.

You can learn to give yourself the care and kindness you need when things are difficult.

"Kind words can be short and easy to speak, but their echoes are truly endless."

Mother Teresa

How Do You Treat A Friend?

The simplest way to understand and embody self-compassion is to reflect on the following scenarios.

Pause a while and contemplate right now; yes, before you turn another page!

Consider how you treat a close friend who is struggling in some way...

Maybe they have made a right old blunder at work; perhaps they just blew a gasket at their partner or child; or maybe they just failed at something they tried really hard to succeed at...

How do you respond to them?

- 💜 What do you say?

- What tone of voice do you use?

- How do you respond with your body?

- What might change in your body language?

You may like to close your eyes, take your time to see and feel and hear how you are with your friend who is struggling in some way...

Here's a space to write your response if you'd like to... (it helps to clarify your thoughts)

♥   So what was that like to consider how you respond to a friend who was struggling?

♥   Did you get in touch with your tender, kind and compassionate self?

♥   What did you do for them? Did you give them a comforting hug or perhaps make them a soothing cuppa?

♥   Did you offer to listen to them for as long as they needed?

♥   Did you reassure them that they weren't stupid or a failure?

♥   Did you acknowledge that it was actually pretty tough - perhaps that you too would have found it hard?

♥   Was your voice gentle and encouraging?

Mmmm, I wonder if you're much kinder than you give yourself credit for...

Ok, let's consider another scenario. Ready?

Consider how you treat yourself when you are struggling in some way.

Maybe you've made a right old blunder at work: perhaps you just blew a gasket at your partner or child; or maybe you just failed at something you tried really hard to succeed at...

- How do you respond to yourself?

- What do you say to yourself?

- What tone of voice do you use?

- How do you respond with your body?

- What might change in your body language?

You might like to close your eyes again, take your time to see and feel and hear how you treat yourself.

Here's a space to write your response down if you'd like to... (this will help with your reflection later)

💜　　So, what was that like? Pretty gruesome? Pretty shocking? Not very pretty at all really?

💜　　Was there any difference? Did you feel fairly neutral?

There's no right answer and everyone's response is unique.

Many participants in my MSC classes have shared that their internal response to themselves when struggling was starkly different to how they respond to their friends. Their internal responses often sound something like this:

"Suck it up you idiot!"

"WTF did you expect anyway, you loser?"

You're such a dick-head, prat, arse, fool... (fill in the blank.)"

"You can never do anything right."

"You should know better!"

And so on and so on and so on....

You probably wouldn't say many of those words out loud, let alone say them to your best friend! True?

Curious that you are willing to say them to yourself?

And what about your tone? Was it patient and kind; thoughtful and compassionate or was it rather more intolerant and impatient?

Take a moment to compare your two responses. There may be an extreme contrast, (like mine was the first time I did this exercise) or it may not be too different. Remember, there is no right response to this reflection exercise, just a door-opening of awareness as to how you treat yourself compared to how you treat loved ones.

You can pause in this space for a while if that feels like a kind choice...

If you are feeling rather battered and bruised after this exercise, give yourself a moment to consider Kristin's research findings:

Over three quarters of the US population[1] are significantly kinder to others than they are themselves.

If you are one of these 78%, you can soothe yourself with the knowledge that you are not alone.

If you are in the other 22% that's fine too. Please don't beat yourself up either way! We all view these experiences through unique lenses, so you are no better or worse wherever you are on the self-compassion scale. This exercise is simply intended to bring awareness to how we behave inwardly and outwardly, so that we can bring a kinder approach to ourselves no matter what.

If you are still feeling a little raw why not give yourself a little bit of time to gather yourself? Give yourself some breathing space. Give yourself a break, perhaps have a calming cuppa and soothe yourself any way you can - maybe go outside for a stroll and shake off those pesky judgements as you unwind in nature for a while.

Do whatever you can, as best you can, just for now. And when you're ready, I'll be waiting on the next page. Remember you are ok just as you are and you're doing great.

This is the beginning. Take your time...

You can be your
own best friend

Being kind to yourself and treating yourself as you would your bestie, may feel alien to you right now, but hold on bald eagle, this new way of being takes practice and is dose dependent.

When you want big muscles or a toned waist, you get your booty down to the gym and shake it bay-beee, don't you!? Unlike working out, if you want to grow your self-compassion muscles, it's a lot less 'doing' and a lot more 'undoing'!

You do need to practise and it takes commitment to change the self-critical habits of a life-time. It can be done and you too can be your own best friend.

You've got this! So let's begin...

"In the middle of difficulty lies opportunity."

Albert Einstein

The (seemingly) 'bad' news is...

*You are both
the attacker
and the attacked!*

Your brain and body respond as if you are literally being attacked - stress hormones will flood your body. If you are chronically beating yourself up - attacking your sense of self, then I believe this can lead to ill heath.

The (genuinely) 'good' news is...

You can be both the soother and the soothed!

Your brain and body respond as if you are literally being soothed - happy hormones and opiates will flood your body. You will calm your stress response and pacify your nervous system that was in red alert and help return it to balance.

Recognising this, you can embrace this new way of being with confidence and reassurance. Knowing over time that with courage, regular practice and gentle application, you can befriend your beautiful self and be the kind, caring and compassionate friend you are to so many others.

To learn to be kind to yourself, you need to be willing to put down the pick axe that you may have used for many years to hack at yourself and bring a warmer presence to your approach.

Imagine your heart (and all the answers you think you are looking for to 'fix' yourself) is locked inside a giant iceberg. Instead of repeatedly hacking at it with a sharp and painful pick axe that leaves cracks in the ice and unsightly scars, you instead choose to tend to your heart and let the warmth of your own heart gently, slowly and compassionately melt the ice from the inside out.

This way, you no longer have to hurt yourself. Rather you can bring the warmth and kind consideration you bring to others, to yourself. It is slower. It can (and usually does) create puddles and make a bit of a mess. But in the long term, you will uncover the jewel in your own heart that shines so brightly, it will never freeze over again.

So what needs to happen? What do you need to move towards for you to begin melting your armour and befriending yourself?

Befriending yourself

There are 3 components to warming up your critical mind and releasing the harsh thinking habits. According to Kristin Neff's model the three components to mindful self-compassion are:

Mindfulness
Self-kindness
Common Humanity

Ready to dive in? Nice deep breath.

Here we go...

Mindfulness

First you need to notice that you are struggling. Mindfulness helps us notice what is happening, rather than being on auto pilot. Much of the time, we are so busy and so distracted we rarely pay attention to the present moment. You can begin to hone your awareness about how you are treating yourself, how you are speaking to yourself and how it feels.

With a mindful approach, you do your best to let go of the judge and jury inside your head and meet the tough stuff with a balanced, non-judgemental attitude.

Mindfulness helps you move toward and 'be with' the painful, tough stuff just as it is, with a balanced state of awareness. There is no longer a need to suppress the feelings, avoid or push against what is going on.

When you struggle, fail to meet your (often very high) expectations or experience feeling stupid, you can find it hard to be mindful. It is easier to lose your temper, distract or busy yourself or eat, drink or chat your way out of your emotional discomfort.

You may begin to notice that you can often get carried away with your negative 'broken record' thinking with stories of 'poor me and my messed up, imperfect life'. That's ok, this is part of the journey.

These self-imposed barriers can begin to melt as you bring your attention and good intention to your suffering.

When you begin to notice your habits of thought and behaviour with an accepting and friendlier disposition, you can unravel the patterns and bring a new, compassionate approach into your life.

"Mindfulness isn't difficult. We just need to remember to do it!"

Sharon Saltzberg

Is your mind full
or
are you mindful?

Self-Kindness

Once you have noticed you are struggling, you can give yourself what you need, starting with kindness. You can practise giving yourself the same tenderness, reassurance and compassion you would give to your loved ones.

This is your antidote to the self-judgement, the mean commentary and the cruel sniping you may have habitually experienced.

As you begin to flex your self-kindness muscles, you gently melt the inner critic and befriend the noise that in the past may have paralyzed you.

When you begin to bring kindness to yourself and your response to difficult circumstances, you become an ally, rather than an enemy.

Western culture places great emphasis on being kind to others, giving to others, helping others and to give rather than receive. However...

...you cannot give from an empty cup!

You need to take the oxygen first. Being 'unconscious' (grumpy, judgemental, self-critical) does not help bring balance into your life or your relationships and does not increase your kindness to others.

Self-compassion invites you to treat yourself as you would others. You can learn to stop beating yourself up when you make a mistake and respond with kindness.

We will explore how to do this in a little while...

"Close your eyes.
Fall in love.
Stay there."

Rumi

Common Humanity

Common humanity helps you embrace a bigger picture approach to life. You begin to recognise that everyone struggles sometimes and that this is natural. It helps begin to melt any stories that you might have made up that everyone else has got their life sorted and is leading perfect lives (social media can often portray very misleading perspectives of other people's lives, when what we are seeing is the selected rose-tinted version - it is not the whole picture).

When you believe your big bad self: that you are the only one who is flawed in the whole human race; that you are the only one that cannot quite manage to be perfect or successful (by whatever measure you are judging yourself), then you have the tendency to isolate yourself. You hide. When you fail or feel stuck in a rut, you push against it and buy into the story that you are abnormal in your struggle.

Instead of isolating and judging yourself, you can bring a new, healthy wholesome belief into your gorgeous, precious heart (and mind) and embrace the following thinking. It sounds something like this...

"If anyone else was walking in my shoes right now, with the challenges I am facing, with the history I am carrying, then they too would probably find this tough."

And there you have it. You are officially no longer an alien, you are fully human instead!

P.S. A note about being the same and yet different

We are all fingerprint unique, that's what makes us special. However, we all share a common thread. We are all human. We all have the same basic needs.

We all have the desire to be loved and accepted for who we are, just as we are!

"We are all connected.
What unites us is our
common humanity.
White, black, rich, poor,
Christian, Muslim
or Jew – pain is
pain – joy is joy."

Desmond Tutu

"If you want
others to be happy,
practice compassion.

If you want to be happy,
practice compassion."

Dalai Lama

Opening & Closing

As you bumble perfectly imperfectly along this self-compassion path, you will undoubtedly meet some bumps in the road. This is perfectly natural. As you deepen your awareness of your thoughts, feelings and behaviours, it can become a little overwhelming. When this happens you can continue to take great care of yourself as you would a dear friend who is feeling overwhelmed.

The easiest way to describe how you can keep yourself feeling safe when your cup feels full or overflowing, is by 'closing'. Imagine a tap. You are in charge of the flow. You cannot control the water pressure, but you can choose how much you open or close the tap.

You have 100% permission to open or close as much or as little as you need to as you embark on your self-compassion adventure. This is a genuine kindness to keep yourself safe as you explore unfamiliar territory.

Whenever it starts to feel too much, simply choose to close your emotional 'tap'. You don't need the water to be gushing out at full blast. Remember you are in charge of the flow. A gentle trickle may be more than enough as you learn new ideas and new ways of being with yourself.

You can 'close' by simply taking your thoughts else-where. A spot of daydreaming can do the trick or finding the wallpaper suddenly rather interesting. You may find yourself sleepy or tired. That's ok and natural. Take a nap. It may be the kindest choice. You may also find yourself wearing grumpy trou-sers - getting annoyed can be the perfect way for you to 'close' if things are getting too difficult to meet in that moment. Know whatever you choose to do to enable you to 'close' is just fine. Give your-self permission to 'close'. You don't need to push yourself with this new compassionate way of life. Striving is not kind. Let it go for now. You'll meet whatever you need to when you are ready. You're doing great.

Similarly, if you want to open and you feel strong and clear, steady in your compassionate seat, then by all means, open your tap as much as you wish. Welcome the tears, the laughter, the strong emotions and the sensations that may arise as you open your floodgates to your experience.

The most important thing to remember is that *you are in charge of your tap.* You are in charge of the flow. You are in charge of your experience in every moment as best you can be. Keep your tap flowing at a rate that you feel comfortable and safe with.

Backdraft!

Ironically, you can feel really unsettled, overwhelmed or upset when you first give yourself kindness and truly allow yourself to receive self-compassion. It can be such a new and foreign experience that it may catch you by surprise and knock you right off your feet. Please be reassured that this too is perfectly natural.

Curiously, when we begin to give ourselves what we need, it can feel like the self-compassion is actually making us feel worse. This is not the case, but it sure feels uncomfortable. Please know you're ok to feel this and it's a perfectly natural response even if it feels rather unpleasant in the moment.

When your heart is blazing with self-hatred, self-loathing or self-doubt, kind and sympathetic words can crack open the door to your heart and the pain inside will leak out and feel like it is burning you. This is known as backdraft.

Have you ever had a really abysmal day and you're just managing to hold yourself together when a colleague or friend comes up to you, gives you a warm smile, perhaps puts a kind hand of reassurance on your shoulder and asks if you're ok? Have you ever responded with *"please, whatever you do, don't be nice to me right now or I'll cry!"*? Sometimes, just the gesture of someone being nice to you when you are struggling is enough to make you leak buckets.

Likewise, when you give yourself kindness it can feel painful. As described by Christopher Germer and Kristin Neff, *"Backdraft refers to the pain (often very old pain) that may arise when you give yourself warmth, affection, kindness and compassion."*

Consider a fire raging in a room and the door is closed, the fire remains contained. When the door is opened and more oxygen rushes in to feed the fire, the flames expand and rage through the house. This is what emotional backdraft can feel like.

Firefighters drill small holes in the windows and doors to control and contain the fire. This is why you are encouraged to go slowly as you learn to be self-compassionate and only touch the heat of your suffering a little bit at a time. This way, you can apply the salve of kindness in good measure as you meet the warmth of your own heart.

Remember, the feelings of overwhelm are not created by self-compassion: we are allowing the pain we may have stuffed down for decades to be set free.

Backdraft is a healing process and, whilst it may feel uncomfortable, it will transform old wounds and heal them. This is why you are invited to be a slow learner. Go gently my friend. You are on the self-compassion path now. All is well.

Your Critical Voice

You may be surprised by what I'm going to suggest next, so do your best to stay open and know that if you 'close' and resist these suggestions, that too is perfectly fine. It will all unfold perfectly, as and when you are ready. Remember you are safe to feel whatever comes up and you have permission to 'close' if you need to. Go at your own pace. You can revisit this when you are ready.

Although your self-critical voice often causes you pain and distress, it is worth getting to know it better. I promise you, this will be helpful.

Your critical voice may not be the vicious, cruel enemy that you've always believed it to be. If you were to press pause on your automatic judgement of the so-called enemy inside your head for a moment and open your mind to a new possibility, I wonder what you might discover.

Ok, so here goes...

What helpful or constructive purpose might your critical voice be serving? Yes, I am asking you to consider that seemingly cruel and perhaps vicious voice might actually be serving a positive purpose. It may be offering you something valuable you have never considered.

Take a moment to reflect how your critical voice might be trying to help you... Go on, you can do it. You may like to close your eyes, take a few slow, deep breaths and open to the possibility that your critical voice might be on your side. Here's a little space to write if you'd like to...

What did you discover?

💜 Perhaps you uncovered a voice that was trying to motivate you to be your best?

💜 Perhaps you recognised that an internal critical voice might be less painful than receiving external criticism?

💜 Perhaps the enemy inside your head that bangs on about you not being good enough, might well be trying to protect you by keeping your expectations low - so you don't feel disappointed?

💜 Perhaps hearing your internal voice of criticism keeps you part of the clan, so that you feel like you fit in and have a place in the world?

If you couldn't find any positive benefits to this inner critical voice, you may like to consider it could simply be trying to *keep you safe.*

Now I'm not saying it has a particularly helpful, kind or constructive way of going about keeping you safe. All I am suggesting is that you might like to consider it's intention may have been good and it may have always been doing its best for you.

What if your critical voice was actually (as one of my participants described) your personal bodyguard?

Turning towards your inner critic can be very painful, especially if you have believed it was your enemy all your life. Go slowly and approach this with care and compassion.

In the early days, you may like to consider negotiating with your inner critic. Your inner critic has done a stirling job of keeping you safe, by whatever means (whether you deem it helpful or unhelpful). Just like a frightened child, it may need some gentle reassurance that it is safe to change its tone. Tread slowly and gently. Respect the survival mechanism of your inner critic. You may like to explore softening your approach to this previously perceived enemy inside your head. Perhaps you could soften your tone, strike up a conversation and ask it a few gentle questions...

💜   How would it be if we tried a different way?

💜   How would it be if you eased up on the critical tone?

💜   What if we could work together to find a new way to feel safe and secure?

Over time, with patience and practice, you will begin to have a lighter relationship with your inner critic when it surfaces...

"Ahhh, I see you!"

"What monkey business are you up to?"

"You are being cheeky/mean/troublesome today!"

"Your inner critic is simply a part of you that needs more self-love."

Amy Leigh Mercree

Remember, this is a *little* book of self-compassion. It is a toe-dip into exploring possibilities of being kinder to yourself and befriending all parts of you, including your critical part. Take it gently and slowly and if you really want to befriend the perceived enemy inside your head, I highly recommend you embark on the Mindful Self-Compassion training with a skilled teacher who can guide and support you on this life-transforming adventure...

Soft Landing

So here you are. You've made it this far. You're doing great! Before we embark on any more learning adventures, I think it is time to experience a soft landing...

A soft landing is simply a warm and gentle opportunity to press pause on the busyness of the day and take a moment for yourself; to enter the present moment with fresh eyes and a warm heart.

It is a tender and kind way to transition from one experience to the next: arriving at work after a traffic-filled journey; beginning a meeting; starting a new conversation; getting home after a long day. All these are wonderful opportunities to press pause and 'be with' yourself and the present moment, just for a moment.

You can simply sit still for a moment. You can take a few slow, smooth, deep breaths and watch your breathing for a little while. You can observe the sound of the kettle as you wait for it to boil. It doesn't matter what you do, or rather not do. It is a

simple and elegant way to gently and kindly 'land' in the moment.

How often do you rush from one thing to the next, no time to even take a breath before the next demand crashes into your lap? On and on you go, without a moment even to catch your breath. So for now, enjoy the space on this page. This can be your soft landing pad! Return to it whenever you feel the need to rest, reflect or simply take a break and hang out with your new-found friend - yourself!

"We need a small space
where we can take
care of our nervous
system and restore our
tranquility and peace."

Thich Nhat Hanh

Your Compassionate Voice

When exploring how you 'treat a friend', what did your voice sound like when offering support and kindness to your close friend? You probably used soft and gentle tones, wanting to soothe and reassure your friend. You probably wanted the best for them; wanted to offer them comfort and solace. You probably listened compassionately and didn't interrupt them; just allowed them to empty out their troubles. You probably did everything you could to bring relief by being fully present with them.

Even though you may not have wholly received or listened to your compassionate voice, it has always been there. How you treat a friend demonstrates just how awesome you are at offering kindness and comfort to others. It is a very wise and understanding part of you. It loves you unconditionally and desires the best for you.

"Unlike self-criticism,
which asks if you're
good enough,
self-compassion asks
what's good for you?"

Kristin Neff

It is time to listen to your compassionate voice, even just for a moment, and begin to receive the loving kindness it has naturally bestowed on others.

Remember, this is a little step in a big adventure. Go slowly and gently and remember to turn your tap to the flow you feel comfortable with.

If you would like to, you can put your adventurous boots on, place your binoculars around your neck and pack your little rucksack, ready for your first expedition into the realm of self-compassion. Ensure you have time and space to explore this reflection and then settle in with curiosity.

So, when you are ready, turn the page and let's begin...

Think of a behaviour that you often beat yourself up about. Not a biggie, just something that you would ideally like to change. Keep it simple and doable - such as I don't meditate regularly, or I over indulge when I'm tired, or I don't give my body enough exercise or sleep.

You will undoubtedly know straight away what your critical voice would say about this behaviour and the unkind and unhelpful tone it would use. If you need to, let the critical voice spew out its tirade and then press pause on the exercise and rest for a moment.

When you are ready, reflect on the same situation but, this time, consider how your compassionate voice responds.

Give yourself time and space to reflect on the kind and soothing voice that wants the best for you; wants you to be happy and free from suffering.

If it feels comforting to do so, spend some time tuning into your compassionate voice and write a letter to yourself from your compassionate voice. Let its wisdom and kindness flow onto the page without editing or critiquing the kind words that arrive.

Now, if this feels too hard or out of reach right now, why not try writing a letter to a close friend who is struggling with the same situation. This will help you practise accessing and hearing your compassionate voice.

Dear...

*With love and support from
your Compassionate Voice*

♥

Your in-built antidote to the inner critical voice

Consider mummy cat taking care of her new-born kittens. She keeps them warm, safe and soothed. She protects them with her body, wrapping herself around her vulnerable young. She keeps them warm by keeping them close. She soothes and reassures them with her purring.

Mummy cat demonstrates physical ways to relax and calm her developing young. Soothing touch and gentle vocalisation have been shown[3] to activate the mammalian caregiving system. Anecdotally, I would propose that warmth also brings comfort when you are feeling vulnerable or in a pickle.

Therefore three ways to bring yourself comfort are:

- ♥ Soothing touch

- ♥ Gentle vocalisations

- ♥ Physical warmth

What's magical about the mammalian caregiving system is that you don't have to think about it. As a mammal you are already hard-wired, pre-programmed to respond to these triggers.

When you receive a hug, your body responds; happy hormones (oxytocin, the so called 'love hormone') is released so that you experience the 'warm and fuzzies' that come with this physical gesture of soothing touch.

You probably don't need me to convince you that a warming cup of hot choc after a tough day or coming in from the cold into a cozy, warm house is also very soothing. And if you think about a time when you were a tiddly peep, fell over and hurt yourself, you were hopefully reassured by a caring adult with a soft and kind voice as they picked you up and gently tended to your grazed knee.

Now this mammalian caregiving system doesn't switch off just because you're no longer knee high to a grasshopper. It stays with you for life. Even when you are old and wrinkly your body will still be soothed and comforted by a tender stroke of your hand, being wrapped in a warm blanket or by being comforted by soft and gentle vocalisations.

This is very good news for you! This natural and integral part of you can bring solace and comfort whenever you need it. Whether something outside your control has just happened, like someone has just driven into the back of your shiny new car, or whether it's your inner critic having a field day blasting you with all sorts of obscenities because you've made a mistake - your mammalian caregiving system can help you return to a safe and calm place.

You can give this to yourself! You can nurture and develop your ability to give yourself what you need in times of stress by providing warmth, soothing and supportive touch and gentle vocalisations.

Let's practise...

" Be kind whenever possible.
It is always possible."

Dalai Lama

Soothing and supportive touch...

Giving yourself the physical gesture of self-compassion.

It may seem strange to suggest you learn to comfort yourself with a soothing gesture in times of stress, but it really does work. You are actively soothing yourself in a moment of difficulty. You become both the soother and the soothed. You do not have to rely on anyone else to bring you comfort, you can give it to yourself. Imagine a friend is holding your hand and giving you a squeeze of encouragement and courage in a troublesome moment.

What if you could give this reassurance and support to yourself? In a curious kind of way, you will never feel alone again when you practise this physical act of self-kindness.

Why not plug into this little meditative soothing touch practice to help you explore where you receive the most soothing in your body?

Here's the written outline if you'd like to understand what you are going to embark on, before you
give it a go and listen to the audio:

Find a nice comfortable position, either
sitting or lying. Ensure your body, especially your spine is supported.

Enjoy a few slow, smooth breaths to help
you settle and come to the present moment.

When you feel ready, choose your first
physical gesture, such as gently placing one
hand on your cheek or resting your hands
on your tummy. You may like to move your
hand or hands gently in a circular motion,
softly stroking your chosen place. Notice
how this makes you feel and how your
body responds to this kind attention.

Notice your active hand stroking, sooth-ing or holding as the soother. Then notice your body being stroked, soothed and held as the receiver (being soothed). How does it feel to recognise you are both the sooth-er and the soothed?

When you feel complete with the first ges-ture simply move on to another place; per-haps gently stroking your arms in a self-hug or placing your hands over your heart.

Spend as much time as you desire in each position, being curious as to how you feel when you give yourself this soothing touch.

Continue to experiment with other areas; gently stroking the back of one hand, cup-ping your hands around your face or gently giving yourself a squeeze.

When you feel complete, consider which part of your body felt the most responsive place. Enjoy giving this place a little more soothing touch for a while.

Rest here.

Gentle Voice

Remember how your critical voice yapped at you the last time you made a mistake, made a fool of yourself or when you simply didn't understand something? Well this is not the voice that you need to soothe you!

Recall that time when you were little, and you fell over and grazed your knee. Remember the kind friend or adult who helped pick you up, dusted you off and reassured you that you were going to be alright? Remember the way they spoke to you?

"Are you ok? Oh, dear let's see what's happened here? Oh my, that is a nasty graze..."

Whatever words they used, it was all offered with a gentle tone. Their voice was tender and softly spoken.

This is the voice you can cultivate inside your own head when you are hurting.

Warmth

Next time you notice you are cold (there's your mindfulness), recognise how tense your body may be feeling.

What if your body was your best friend? Would you leave your bestie shivering and with teeth chattering or would you find a lovely warm blanket and maybe even a hot water bottle to soothe your friend by wrapping them up?

Now it's time to practise this for yourself and give this to your body. Even if it's simply that your toes have got cold, why not make the effort to pop on some soft, fluffy socks or warming slippers and soothe yourself with this simple yet kind gesture?

Objection Your Honour!!!

If the judge inside your head is barking on that you are a selfish, self-pitying, self-indulgent, weakling who just wants to be a sloth because you don't want to push yourself anymore to shift your lazy butt off the couch, then perhaps offer the judge and jury inside your head the evidence that the prosecution has clearly overlooked!

Self-compassionate people are more likely to...

♥ engage in healthier behaviours like drinking less, exercising and eating well

♥ take greater responsibility for their actions and are more likely to apologise if they offend someone

♥ be less afraid of failure and are more likely to try again and persist in their efforts after failing

♥ cope with tough situations like trauma, divorce and chronic pain

♥ engage in perspective-taking and to realise they are not alone in their experience

♥ compromise in relationship conflicts and be more compassionate towards others

So, just to be clear...

If you are kind to yourself or if you begin to bring a compassionate approach to your life and living...

- You are NOT selfish!

- You are NOT self-indulgent!

- You are NOT weak!

- You are NOT self-pitying!

- You are NOT lazy!

- You are NOT unmotivated!

- You are more likely to cope with the tough stuff that arises in your everyday life.

- You are more likely to manage difficult situations and difficult people with more compassion.

- You are more likely to look on the bright side when you fail or make a mistake.

- You will be more resilient inside your own head and will waste of lot less energy beating yourself up for being imperfect, for being human.

The defence rests your honour!

"Self-care means giving the world the best of you, instead of what is left of you."

Katie Reed

The 2 sides of self-compassion

This self-compassion stuff is not just all soft and fluffy you know. It takes a courageous person to embark on meeting and changing a monstrous habit of a lifetime. It takes a brave soul to address the feelings he or she may have ingeniously stuffed down and avoided most of their life. It takes a daring fellow to stare into the tiger's mouth and meet the critical voice with patience and composure.

Consider a person who has suffered domestic violence. Theirs is the valiant heart that learns to say "NO!" to the hand that beats them or the situation they are in. They learn to be self-compassionate enough to develop skills to build safety for themselves (and often their children).

Consider the paramedic who risks their life to save another or the teacher who works out of hours with no extra pay to ensure their students reach their potential. These too are powerfully compassionate acts. It is important, before we begin sharing the message of self-compassion, that we recognise the Yin & Yang of Self-Compassion.

The Yin of self-compassion is inward facing; this is primarily focused on 'being with' ourselves in a kind and compassionate way. We comfort, soothe and validate ourselves.

The Yang of self-compassion is outward facing; this is primarily focused on 'acting in the world'. We protect, provide and motivate ourselves.

It is helpful to recognise both sides of self-compassion have potent parts to play in our inner life and that both are equally valuable. Self-compassion can flow through your life whether you are offering yourself comfort in a painful situation or if you are protecting yourself from danger with a firm 'no!'

No matter which side of self-compassion you are being guided by, you will be practising a friendly and caring attitude.

Learning to be your own best friend is the key: asking yourself the imperative question:

"What do I need?"

This will serve you to the highest, even if you cannot answer the question immediately or have limited means to meet your needs in that moment.

"Talk to yourself
like you would to
someone you love."

Brene Brown

Golden Goodness of Self-Compassion

This little book would not be complete without a wee mention of the ancient art of Kintsugi. It means golden joinery. It is the japanese art of repairing broken pottery with lacquer dusted or mixed with powdered gold, silver or platinum. Its philosophy approaches brokenness and subsequent repair as part of the history of the object - rather than something to hide or disguise. It embraces the belief that nothing is ever truly broken.

If your heart has been broken and the scars that you'd healed were still visible on the outside, how powerful and beautiful would it be to decorate those wounds with gold? You would be demonstrating your resilience that you have faced a difficult situation and survived. You would be highlighting your courage rather than trying to mask the scar.

Similarly, all the times your body has been injured or broken. Rather than trying to cover up the scars (I have a rather large one on my throat) how powerful would it be to adorn your scars, wrinkles, stretch marks and blemishes with gold, celebrating your remarkable strength and durability to physical challenge.

Western society is so obsessed with perfection.

♥ What if you celebrated your flaws, your perceived mistakes and your imperfections as places of growth; pronouncement of your humanness and commemoration of your common humanity?

♥ What if you stopped hiding? What if you stopped being ashamed of your perceived faults and weakness and stood tall in your messy life?

Still a little bit crazy, a little bit moody, a little bit forgetful... Still a little bit judgemental, a little bit impatient and a little bit envious... And yet you would be true and real, honest and courageous.

A compassionate mess!

"The goal of practice is to become a compassionate mess. That means fully human – often struggling, uncertain, confused – with great compassion."

Rob Nairn

♥ What if you could embrace all parts of you?

♥ What if you judged yourself a little bit less and cared for yourself a little bit more?

♥ What if you looked in the mirror and saw golden acceptance shining through your tears instead of self-criticism?

So whenever you catch yourself saying, "I'm too fat, I'm too thin, I'm a weakling or I'm just plain stupid", why not administer the healing balm of self-compassionate golden glue to every judgement that may have caused a crack in your heart and mind?

♥ In time you will recognise you are way more valuable with your golden scars than if you had led a seemingly perfect (and possibly boring) life!

"The point is...
not to try to throw
ourselves away and
become something better.

It's about befriending
who we already are."

Pema Chödrön

The Kindest Thing...

This is my most favourite question and one that I have frequently asked myself since learning the mindful art of self-compassion:

What's the kindest thing I can do for myself right now?

If you close this little book with nothing else in your head or heart except this question, then the self-compassion seed will have been sown!

If you're up to your eyeballs in *'brown stuff'*, if your world has just been turned upside down or if your heart has just been shattered into a thousand pieces, simply offer yourself this question:

What's the kindest thing I can do for myself right now?

Repeat it with me now, to engrave it into your mind and heart...

What's the kindest thing I can do for myself right now?

What's the kindest thing I can do for myself right now?

What's the kindest thing I can do for myself right now?

In times of trouble, do your best to ask yourself this question. You can practise by asking your loved ones the same question when they hit a wall, metaphorically speaking. It will help reinforce the good intention in times of trouble.

What's the kindest thing I can do for myself right now?

It may simply be that you take a break. It might be that you go outside or leave the troubling space. You may well choose to phone a friend, have a shower or make a cuppa. It doesn't matter what the act of kindness is. What is fundamentally crucial is that you are offering yourself the time and space to honour yourself. You are putting you back into the equation of your life. You are being kind to the one you go home with. In so doing your self-compassionate life will begin to blossom.

If you forget, which in the early days is a high possibility, there's no need to beat yourself up when you realise you could've, should've, but didn't ask yourself. It's simply another opportunity to practise self-compassion.

Remember, self-compassion practice is dose-dependent. The more you practise the more you will remember to be self-compassionate. The more you remember, the more self-compassionate you will become. And so the upward self-kindness cycle will evolve.

At Kind Mind Academy, the lovely Liz Walker (fellow MSC teacher, logistics queen and all-round kindness superstar) decided to bring this question to life for our graduates by creating a little bracelet with this magical question on.

What's the kindest thing I can do for myself right now?

Wear your kindness bracelet with pride. It will remind you to be kind to yourself in difficult times. It might also ignite many a conversation for the curious heart who may very well be ready to hear the message of self-compassion.

And when the time is right, (and you'll know when) you will be with someone who needs your bracelet more than you do. Please pay it forward. Share the message of mindful self-compassion. Give them your bracelet, your warm encouragement and bucket loads of kindness as you reassure them there is another way to live inside their own head:

A kind way

A compassionate way

A friendly way...

Starting place

There is so much more we can explore about self-compassion. But if we did, it would no longer be a *'little'* book! If it was a big book, chances are you wouldn't pick it up and read it. And anyway, your inner critic probably wouldn't give you that much time to devote to yourself - so 'little' it will remain.

Please remember, this little book is a starting place. It is a gentle springboard from which you can launch yourself into the world of living self-compassionately. It is not the holy grail (well not the entire holy grail), but by golly it is a delicious taste of the way it could be if you embraced a kinder way of living inside your own skin.

Self-compassion also entails embodying our core values, self-appreciation, gratitude and ways to cultivate happiness. There are silver linings we can adopt, and we can foster a deeper understanding of our unmet needs. But we will leave these for another day...

Thank you for reaching the end of this little book. I hope it will be the beginning of something magical and miraculous for you to nuzzle in to, so that you can live your extraordinary life with self-kindness leading the way. There is much to practise, but for now:

Start with one little intention...

Start with one little step...

Start with one little act of kindness...

"The curious paradox of life is that when I accept myself just as I am, then I can change."

Carl Rogers

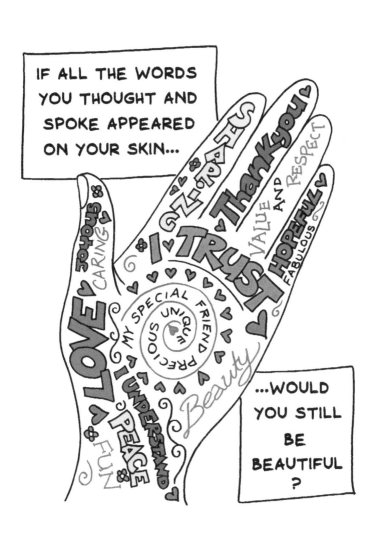

Find out more

You can download some free guided meditations to help you embark on your self-compassionate adventure. Visit:

www.TheLittleBookOfSelfCompassion.com

If you'd like to learn more about Mindful Self-Compassion and the range of courses offered by Kind Mind Academy in the UK, Australia, New Zealand and other heavenly places, visit us at:

www.KindMindAcademy.com

If you'd like to order a Kindness Bracelet for yourself, a loved one or your entire organisation, you are warmly invited to go to www.KindnessBand.com

If you fancy being inspired by Kind Mind Academy's MSC alumni and view other fantastic and informative videos, you can enjoy Kind Mind Academy's You Tube channel with a nice warming cuppa and maybe some popcorn! Visit:

www.YouTube.com/c/KindMindAcademy

If you would like to continue your *'little'* steps, you can join Kathryn on Kind Mind Academy's Facebook page for her #MSCBitesize live each week.

www.Facebook.com/KindMindAcademy

#MSCBitesize explores mindful self-compassion in everyday life in bite size chunks! This way you can continue your MSC adventure without being over-whelmed. (And if it's crazy o'clock in your part of the world, you can watch the recording and leave comments and questions as desired.)

If you would like to explore where you can learn the life-changing skills of MSC in your country, simply visit www.CenterForMSC.org where you will find everything you need to know about the incredible work Kristin, Chris, Steve, Michelle and all their trained teachers are providing across the globe.

If you are wondering how self-compassionate you are, you may like to explore Kristin Neff's Self-Compassion Scale. This scale measures your approach to being kind to yourself, how mindful you are in your moments of struggle and your sense of common humanity when facing your flaws or imperfection. Visit www.SelfCompassionScale.com

References

Appendix A

The following elements and concepts of this book are adapted from and inspired by the Mindful Self-Compassion programme developed by Kristin Neff and Christopher Germer. (*Neff, K. & Germer, C. (2018). The Mindful Self-Compassion Workbook. New York: Guilford Press.*) Reprinted with permission of Guilford Press.

p16 Soothing Soup/Flu analogy (*Chapter 13 – Stages of Progress – Page 95*)

p20 How do you treat a friend? (*Chapter 1 – What is Self-Compassion? – Pages 12-18*)

p34 Brain and Body response (*Chapter 4 – The Physiology of Self-Criticism and Self-Compassion – Page 31*)

p41 Three Components of Mindful Self-Compassion (*Chapter 1 – What is Self-Compassion? – Pages 10-12*)

p56 Opening and Closing (*Introduction – Page 6*)

p60 Backdraft (*Chapter 8 – Backdraft – Pages 57-58. First cited by Germer, C. (2009), The Mindful Path of Self-Compassion pages 150-152*)

Appendix B

p28 1) Kristin Neff (2016)

p71 2) Mindful Self-Compassion Training
www.CenterForMSC.org

p84 3) Stellar & Keltner (2014)

p91 4) Soothing Touch audio download
www.TheLittleBookOfSelfCompassion.com

p113 5) www.KindnessBand.com

Praise for "The Little Book..."

Within the covers of this little book, Kathryn Lovewell has captured the healing essence of self-compassion training. It is not a quick fix, nor is it about being soft when we need to be strong. When we learn to be self-compassionate, we become a genuinely caring and supportive companion to ourselves. Written in a warm and inviting style, with charming illustrations, this book is a great way to begin the journey. You may never look back!

Christopher Germer, PhD
Co-developer, *Mindful Self-Compassion Training*
Author, *The Mindful Path to Self-Compassion*
Lecturer on Psychiatry (part-time), Harvard Medical School

The book may be little, but self-compassion is a big deal. Extensive research has shown that self-compassion makes us more resilient, better able to cope and contributes to our overall well-being. But you will only discover its benefits if you try it. Self-compassion is a simple thing, but not so easy, and this little book is an accessible and delightful invitation into meeting yourself with more warmth, kindness and compassion, especially when you face difficulty, hardship and struggle. Written in the warm-hearted and generous tone of its author, this little book could be your best next step on the road to befriending yourself and finding ease in your life.

Steven D.Hickman, Psy.D.
Executive Director, Center for Mindful Self-Compassion
Founding Director, UC San Diego Center for Mindfulness
Clinical Psychologist

Kathryn Lovewell is a warm-hearted, authentic and skilful teacher of Mindful Self-Compassion. Her gentleness and humanity really shine through in this little book, making it a truly welcoming entry point for those new to self-compassion. I also see this book as a useful resource for those who are already on the 'adventure' of living a more mindful and compassionate life. It is a welcome addition to the ground-breaking work of Drs. Germer and Neff. Thank you Kathryn!

Tina Gibson
Certified MSC Teacher, International Teacher Trainer & Mentor, Center for Mindful Self-Compassion
Director, Adelaide Mindfulness

How do we tame our self-critical voice and become our own best friend? This friendly and practical guide is the ideal place to begin. Through engaging storytelling, Kathryn Lovewell lays out a roadmap for the self-compassion journey. Grab a copy of this mighty little book for your sister, your mom, and your dearest friends, and embark on a life-changing adventure back to your own good heart.

Aimee Eckhardt
Communications Manager, Center for Mindful Self-Compassion
MSC Teacher, Developer of the MSC *Community for Deepening Practice*

"Love and compassion are necessities, not luxuries. Without them humanity cannot survive."

Dalai Lama

About the
Author

Kathryn Lovewell is a passionate Certified Mindful Self-Compassion teacher. She first experienced MSC in 2015 after a long and deep search for self-love, self-acceptance and peace with her body. MSC was the key she had been looking for.

Since that day, every challenge, every moment of pain, every sadness has been an opportunity to practice MSC and come home to kindness.

Kathryn is an award winning emotional health and wellbeing specialist. Since 2006 she has combined meditation, mindful awareness, therapeutic practices and positive psychology to create personal and professional development programmes in the UK, USA & Australia.

She is the author of the bestselling book *Every Teacher Matters; Inspiring Wellbeing through Mindfulness* and co-author of *The Positive Edge Journal*. Her mission is to inspire tender self-care and loving self-kindness across the globe.

Lightning Source UK Ltd.
Milton Keynes UK
UKHW051919171019
351794UK00005B/151/P